The Importance of *Doing* It

*How to Utilize Discipline to Get Out of Bed,
and Make Your Dreams Come True!
A Guide to Taking Action to
Create Successful Habits,
Reduce Stress, Anxiety, & Depression &
Gain Self-Discipline, Motivation, & Success!*

Original Edition

Sage Wilcox

The Importance of Doing It
How to Utilize Discipline to Get Out of Bed, and Make Your Dreams Come True! A Guide to Taking Action to Create Successful Habits, Reduce Stress, Anxiety, & Depression & Gain Self-Discipline, Motivation, & Success!

Copyright © 2016 Sage Wilcox

First Edition

All rights reserved. No part of this book may be reproduced, stored in a retrieval system or transmitted in any form or by any means, electronic, mechanical, photocopying, recording, or otherwise, without the written permission of the publisher.

ISBN-13: 978-1-945290-08-4

ISBN-10: 1-945290-08-0

Library of Congress Control Number: 2016954208

Printed in the United States of America.

DEDICATION

This is dedicated to all of the people who are working hard to better themselves and their situations, day by day, and in every way. Perseverance and discipline pays off. YOU deserve to make your dreams come true and reach your full potential, and this book is for you. Enjoy!

CONTENTS

Acknowledgments... i

Preface... v

Chapters

1. Human Behavior.. 1

    The Ultimate Driver of Human Behavior

    Basic Needs

    Physiological Economics

2. Brain vs. Mind.. 9

    The Brain

    The Mind

    The Psychological Spectrum

3. Forces of the Psyche...................................... 17

    The Juxtaposition

    Separating the Conscious from the Subconscious

    The Human Psyche

    Balance of Forces

4. Recognizing Discipline.................................. 25

    The Three Facets of Discipline

    Behavioral Change Using Discipline

5. Practicing Discipline 31

    Fasting

    Expanding the Practice

6. Success and Discipline 39

    Mindset

    Perception

    Reflection

    Happiness

    Strong Mind

    Habits

7. A Disciplined Life 47

8. Discipline Testimonies 53

    Conclusion 99

    About the Author 103

ACKNOWLEDGMENTS

Deep, humble appreciation to the Divine Source, whom I aspire to grow closer to every day, in faith.

Thanks to all who made this book possible. Also to those who loved and supported me as I worked on getting it published. You know who you are, and I am so appreciative and grateful.

And last but not least, to the readers. Thank you for taking the time to read this book. I hope you enjoy it and find something inside that resonates and inspires you in some way. Thank you. Let's pour our favorite drink, find a comfortable spot, and get started, shall we? Our dreams and goals are waiting to be fulfilled.

Let's not be afraid to speak the common sense truth: you can't have high standards without good discipline.
~ William Hague

PREFACE

As a young child, the word discipline was one of the most disliked words in my budding vocabulary. It was, however, one of my parents and teachers' favorite. I think that word was uttered, spoken, yelled, written and hurled at me many times and on many days. Somehow my parents and teachers just knew how to sow that word into every occasion, be it Christmas dinner, or graduation. It bugged me to no end, but being the shy child that I was, I bit my tongue and accepted it.

It turns out, decades later, that the word has become so ingrained in everything that I do, it happens to be the anchoring reality of my successes and the voice of reason in my failures. As I continuously grow, that word grows with me, giving me insight into what my parents and teachers were conveying when they unceremoniously invoked the word. What I realized after all these years is that the word had one meaning when it left their hearts, and meant something completely different when it pierced mine. Such is the nature of the limitation of speech.

That word and I have come full circle. It's my turn to utter, speak, yell, write and hurl that word at my children now. And the countenance they inevitably wear in the wake of that word crashing into their young hearts is unmistakable. It's the same one I unwittingly paraded all those years ago.

Although it tugs at my heartstrings to see their faces when that word drops like a judge's gavel at the end of sentence pronouncement, I know it's a lesson I have to teach them, because that is the word, among a short list of other words, that will serve as their guide and their guard long after I am no longer here to fill those roles.

As far as success goes, it has come relatively easily because the hard work that needs to be done to achieve anything in life has been done with unrelenting discipline.

It never occurred to me to do anything without it and in turn, discipline has become a habit. Growing up, there were circumstances that forced me to work hard. I had a full-time job when I was 15, all while going to high-school. I had to pay for my school lunches, class ring, senior photos, car, car insurance etc. That's why doing what needed to be done eventually became easy for me.

Because, growing up, I had to learn how to use discipline out of survival, at times it is hard for me to understand why it is so difficult for some people to make discipline a part of their routine or habit. (Yes, you can make discipline a habit.) It is human nature to come up with excuses as to why we don't want to take action. It is human nature to stay in our comfort zones. It takes courage to step beyond what has become the norm for us. But it takes discipline to reach our goals. It takes discipline to become successful. It takes discipline to stay the course. It takes discipline to follow your moral compass. It takes discipline to not let the unlovable make you angry. It takes discipline to get up and go to work each morning. A successful life takes discipline.

This book addresses a number of peripheral issues before honing in on the core substance of discipline itself. It looks at the psychological perspective of discipline as well as the evolutionary perspective and makes the case for balanced discipline. It goes on to lay out the steps of crafting discipline into a habit and again, makes the case for it.

To really get discipline to work for you, you need to know three things. First, you need to know how to recognize it. Second, you need to know how to invoke it. And, third, you need to know what it's not. When you apply this knowledge consistently across the board and you start to recognize the benefits, the habits are reinforced and the positive consequences of discipline begin to manifest in your life.

THE IMPORTANCE OF DOING IT

Like most books of this genre, it would serve you well to approach it repeatedly - meaning, read it more than just once or twice. Much of its secrets, although not intended to be that way, will unlock itself over the course of multiple readings and you will be able to transcend the printed word and appreciate the apparent truth. I assure you that I am not trying to make life difficult for you by presenting it as such. The reason lies in the fact that we speak and communicate using meanings that are not universal. Language leaves the lips of the teacher with one intention yet falls on the ears of the student with a completely different effect. The divergence of the two can only be minimized by repeated exposure and the desire to understand the nature of the subject matter. The same strategy and effect are inherent within the pages of this book.

Discipline, in its simplest form, conveys the measure of the effort required to act on a thought, a decision, or a plan. The verb here does not only mean to physically act, but it can also mean the effort to mentally act, where a person is required to cogitate on something that is not entirely pleasurable or easy to do.

Discipline is not native to our physiology; it is something we learn along the way. Discipline effectively takes the power to act, almost exclusively endowed to our impulses and subliminal thoughts, and transfers it to the logical, reasonable and measured section of our faculties.

At the genesis of our evolution, our brain was only capable of simple thought processes. The brain, at the time, consisted of nothing more than a central nervous system. Our rudimentary control center was more binary in nature allowing only for do - don't do reactions; or yes - no answers. There were no shades of gray, there were no nuances or subtleties. Only one or the other. It was a wild time where the cauldron of nature's ecosystem had endowed our ancestors with a different purpose to life. One where from the day we were born to the day we died, we were some other animal's meal, and some other animal was ours.

There was still no evidence or need for discipline that early in the game. But as the higher functions of the brain we know of today came on line, we were presented with the gift of choice and we had the freedom to choose how we acted when we acted and so on. Our potential choices, analysis, and possible reactions were no longer binary.

While our purpose during the genesis of our species was survival and longevity, our species hasn't changed in its fundamental nature, but the ecosystem we are now a part of has. Since we are but the product of nature we have moved along its changes as a barrel in a raging river. As our original brain tries to adapt its original programming to contemporary conditions, what we are left with are strange outcomes, confusion, and chaos where only rational thought, reflection and the discipline to act help guide us in our daily life.

We are driven by a large measure by our desires, we are constrained by our limitations, and we worry about that which causes fear. All these factors, if not placed in proper context, can disrupt us and make our living a tormented one.

Two things help to shape and smoothen out the course of our journey. First, is our perspective of things; and second, how we react to those perspectives. Our perspective is a function of our mindset, and our reactions are a function of our reasoning. When you bring discipline to bear on both those factors, the host of outcomes take on a more positive shade. As each positive consequence builds on the last positive outcome, you start to make positivity a habit.

You must accept one simple truth, and that is you may not be able to control how nature acts around you, or what others do to you, but you can control how you perceive it and you can control how you react to it, and that alone is enough to change the course of history. And at the core of that positivity and change is discipline.

To understand and invoke discipline in our life, we need to look at its background, how it works and how to invoke it. That is how we present the topic in the rest of the book. We start with the background of human behavior and purpose, and we go on to amalgamate it with how discipline allows you to decide on the right thing to do instead of the easy thing to do, and once you have decided, it shows you how to muster the energy to get it done.

The Importance of *Doing* It

*How to Utilize Discipline to Get Out of Bed,
and Make Your Dreams Come True!
A Guide to Taking Action to
Create Successful Habits,
Reduce Stress, Anxiety, & Depression &
Gain Self-Discipline, Motivation, & Success!*

Original Edition

Sage Wilcox

1
HUMAN BEHAVIOR

What we see as a physical act of a person is a function of, and follows from, the working of the person's mind - whether conscious or subconscious. What begins in the brain as an impulse, fans out into numerous physical steps and movements, and finally results in tangible accomplishment. Each tangible accomplishment then cascades towards a specific purpose.

The concept of a purpose is one that is rather loaded in today's philosophical discourse. But it doesn't have to be here today. The concept of purpose at this stage of the game is fairly simple and can be synthesized down to just one word - living.

The Ultimate Driver of Human Behavior

The fundamental purpose of all living things, be it human, animal, plant, and bacteria is simple - its purpose is to live. That purpose of living transcends space and time. We live in the here and now, and we reproduce to live into the there and tomorrow. Our purpose overcomes the limitations of time by reproduction. So my ancestor from a thousand years ago reaches through time, and even space, to touch my present reality. And a progeny of mine will be my conduit to life sometime in the future. That is the purpose we can see, one we can evidence and one that does not require any stretch of the imagination. We can state it simply here and now for its logic is self-evident. To live invokes divinity and higher meaning as well. We are all worthy and are here for a reason.

With the root of existence deeply entrenched in the rhetoric of life, meaning, and higher truths, we find that the simplest answer to simple questions gets us the most mileage. This simple truth is that we are purposed to live. And that purpose to live is the ultimate driver of human behavior.

Every object on this earth, animate and otherwise, provides evidence that they were just meant to be. To live. To exist. When we take living as the purpose, we then see that every base instinct we have as human beings is to advance that purpose. Then it makes sense why the two most fundamental needs in the world take up so much of our energy and thought to pursue and acquire.

Basic Needs

The basic instinct of the human being is first and foremost to satisfy the basic need - to live and procreate. To live we need to eat and to procreate we need to find a mate and have a family. These are our basic needs. Whatever the basic need, when the body gets it, the brain is rewarded with tremendous pleasure. So when we eat, it's pleasurable. When we find a mate, it's pleasurable. When we engage in sex, it's pleasurable. All because the body rewards the brain for accomplishing what is important towards the primary objective, or the purpose.

The pursuit and consumption of food and sex are the root of everything we do to fill these basic needs, from an instinctual perspective, and this manifests in everything else that goes on in our life. This purpose influences a lot of our decisions, every thought, and action in some direct or indirect way. It even influences our bravado and the depth of fear and ambition; innovation and laziness; initiative and complacency. In essence, this purpose is the driving force behind human behavior. But in today's world, things are a little more complex, times have changed, we have grown and evolved (thankfully), and we can't be running around eating and procreating all day. To counter primal impulses, we need discipline.

But the picture is yet incomplete. There is one more dimension that acts as a catalyst to the human behavior equation. That dimension is the dimension of fear. Fear is a powerful driver in its own right and it can be a powerful motivator as well as a powerful distractor. The only thing that can counter fear is discipline.

But it is deeper than that. This core purpose is encapsulated into our ecosystem. This ecosystem consists of animated and inanimate, living and non-living beings and consists of multiple dimensions which are all balanced. This balance is created within us by opposing forces, where that balance falls is also a function of discipline.

If there comes a choice between living in the present or living perpetually, the body seems to choose the living perpetually. We want to live forever and a lot of times we live as though we will. No doubt that internal design sometimes manifests in people trying to gain immortality. However, the truth is that their body is actually trying to communicate that they live through their progeny down the road. We will live through our descendants, family, and offspring.

Physiological Economics

From a logistics perspective, as well as one from biological economics, there is one currency that we can reduce all effort down to, and that is the currency of energy. The basis of our physiological economics is to balance the supply of energy and the pursuit of goals to achieve our purpose.

We consume food in order to provide the body with energy that can fuel the body, and the operation of systems within the body. The more energy you have the more work you can do, or the longer you can sustain yourself. Think of it this way. If you get a full tank of gas, you can either go a really long distance, or you can make daily trips to the office for more days. We get to choose how we use the full tank of gas.

In the same way, energy in the human equation is rather fungible and compatible, which makes everything more interesting. To hunt and forage for food, you need energy. As such, the economist's calculator in the subconscious part of the brain sets to work by figuring out if the pursuit of the energy (the act of foraging for food), will result in a net positive energy gain. There are times when the pursuit may be so arduous that once you get it, the quarry may not be worth the trouble. Or the quarry may be so small that any effort that is put into it is not worth it because of the opportunity cost, to go after something else, that doesn't have enough calories to make economic sense.

In many cases the body would rather lay dormant, using less energy, while it waits for a larger quarry that doesn't require too much energy to obtain. It's one of the reasons why the lottery is such an appeal to many people - less input effort with the potential for large returns. This is the core structure of the concept of laziness, and it is a powerful driver in the human story.

The point is that the subconscious is relied on to determine if the pursuit of a goal is worth the energy expended and if it is worth it, the next question is could there be an alternative that could be better. This is, in essence, the inner workings of a lazy person or someone who is hesitant or someone who is coming from a place of fear. You see this much of the motivational programs that address the issue of seizing the moment.

THE IMPORTANCE OF DOING IT

The energy equation is a lot more complicated than what has been presented here, but for now, it's important just to know that the entire energy profile of a person does make a difference in how that person fares in his pursuit of an objective.

Built into the energy equation is a buffer. This buffer is there to account for unknown circumstances. Obviously, if a person has a larger buffer, the body kicks into a fear or lazy mode sooner rather than later, and if they have a smaller buffer, they kick into a fear or lazy mode later. This buffer is constructed on historical experience and mindset. If a person is constantly struggling for food, what you find is that they have a larger buffer because the certainty of the next energy source has an uncertainty factor.

As such those with larger buffers, lower energy profiles, and misconceptions of payoff profiles need higher levels of motivation to get the same amount of accomplishment.

I believe in the will. I believe in discipline. I believe in the organization. I believe in the rigor that gives us work. I believe in love as an engine of all things. I believe in the light. I believe in God. I believe in kindness.
~Edgar Ramirez

2
BRAIN VS MIND

Your brain is not your mind. They are two very different things. The first is a physical organ that sits in your cranium, the second is a conceptual framework that uses these different parts of your brain to receive, analyze, store, and output responses.

The Brain

Your brain is the command and control center for all things you consciously will and autonomously control. It is made up of the brainstem, which was the first to form in our evolutionary path; the limbic system, which formed after that; and then there is the cerebrum and the cerebellum. What is interesting is if you look back at the history and evolution of the physical brain, you will find that one of the first to form in the central nervous system was the brainstem.

If you think of the brain in increasing layers of strata, then what you have is the brainstem right at the bottom, and as the other parts of the brain evolved and grew above it. The fear mechanism was hardwired to the rest of the structure and stayed in between the rest of the brain and the control systems of the brain located in the brainstem. This is the reason why fear is such a powerful force in the human development.

Fear does two things we don't realize and it can be an ally, especially when you combine it with discipline. Fear can either freeze you into inaction, or it can energize you into a state of fight or flight. This makes fear an absolute necessity in your quest for success and when used with discipline it can supercharge your efforts. Fear and discipline are necessary for success.

The Mind

The human mind is the nexus between the physical presence of the human body and the spirit of our existence. The mind is malleable, adaptable, flexible and it can be shaped by outside forces. No matter how stubborn the character, or how insistent the behavior, the human condition's greatness lies in its ability to evolve, change and adapt to external forces. The construct that resulted in the development of the human species on top of the rudimentary brain is an amazing accomplishment of nature.

However, the mind is significantly more advanced. It uses decision trees, and statistical inference to come up with possible outcomes and is then able to choose the best scenario. But more importantly, it constantly adjusts when it makes a mistake. The mind lets us learn from our mistakes. In fact, mistakes are the best form of learning because mistakes engage us on many different levels. And this is one of the purposes of psychology. It first sets out seeking the inner workings of the mind by observing the actions that manifest from it; then it goes about understanding itself. The actions that flow from our mind, when observed, are the mirror in which our mind is reflected and we can then get to know it and ourselves better.

As we develop the skills to peer into our actions and see our mind, we find that we have bits and pieces of various traits and characteristics. We all have narcissism, to a certain extent, and empathy to a certain extent. They are both two sides of the same coin. Narcissism looks purely at the welfare of the ego (I plan to do a book on narcissism in the future), while pure empathy is totally altruistic, to the point of self-sacrifice. Neither, at their extremes, is beneficial to the individual or to the species in general. But we are endowed with both traits.

As we grow up, we have impulses to be one or the other and we slowly learn to find the optimal mix of the two. Where and how we are raised plays a huge part into how the two balance out. The ending balance is a function of the environment surrounding us, our upbringing, and our experiences.

But the most important thing in balancing that fine line between narcissism and empathy is what we call discipline. Discipline is the force that pushes against the natural feel to be or do something. In this respect, discipline is a tool. When someone says you have a strong mind, what they are trying to say, aside from the fact that you are sharp, is that your mind is strong enough to overcome impulses, primal instincts, and habits that have adverse consequences. All the things that put someone in control of their actions.

The same goes for all the other traits in psychology. There are two forces defining the extremes and the application of both towards a certain degree determines our character and our temperament.

The Psychological Spectrum

The full spectrum of human psychology spans from precognition and instincts; to logic, reasoning, and intuition; to fear and inaction; to post action cognitive processes that include learning, remorse, memory, gratification and so on. That's a lot of area to cover to understand human psychology, which by definition is the study of the human psyche.

The human psyche seems like the most complex mechanism in the world, but when you begin to understand the human condition in relation to everything around us, the human mind - the subject of human psychology becomes simple to comprehend. It is this simplicity that is one of the dimensions of the mind's power and those who practice the discipline to channel this power will reap the benefits of peace, prosperity, and happiness.

If indeed the pursuit of happiness is your driving motivation, then discipline must be your master.

The difficulty in understanding the human mind arises because the mechanism we use to understand everything in this world, from the growth of fungi to predicting the movement of the stars, is our mind. And within this mind, we are tasked with taking an externally occurring phenomenon and converting it to the point of comprehension and understanding. We do this by the use of notions. But when the mind is asked to study the mind, it becomes almost useless. It's like asking the teeth to chew the teeth, or the nose to sniff itself or the eye to see its cornea. This is essentially the problem we have had from the beginning.

A seemingly tough problem? Not really. The solution is rather simple.

If you want to look into your eye, you can't just use your eye to do it, you need the aid of a mirror. The study of one's self is done in the same conceptual way - through the aid of the concept of reflection - like the reflection in the mirror. That's how the term reflection came about.

THE IMPORTANCE OF DOING IT

If you want to see how the human mind works you have to do it through the process of reflection. This is done by observing the visible manifestations of thought and other processes of the mind. Take for example the observation of a subject voraciously devouring a chicken sandwich. We could deduce that the subject was hungry. Something we could not assume if there wasn't an action to base it on. When we are external to the process, we call that observation. When we take on an external observation personally and look at our own actions, then that becomes an observational reflection.

To be able to advance discipline along an arc that leads to a fulfilled life, the ability to reflect and understand your own inner workings is paramount. Because you need to create discipline habits to counter poor habits and change the trajectory of your life. Without proper reflection, you will not be able to identify the areas of your life that need to be altered.

Talent without discipline is like an octopus on roller skates. There's plenty of movement, but you never know if it's going to be forward, backwards, or sideways.
~ H. Jackson Brown, Jr.

3
FORCES OF THE PSYCHE

Modern humans can be a confused bunch. Not because we are stupid, but rather because we are inherently positioned at the juxtaposition of opposing extremes. As such in one part we are driven by the forces of the tangible and the other part, we are driven by the forces of the intangible. The seen and the unseen. The things we can touch and the things we cannot. And so we spend our lives bouncing between one and the other trying to make sense of it all, when in reality our presence ties one and the other together.

The Juxtaposition

Imagine oil and water. Oil is hydrophobic and as such if left to their own devices, the two will never combine. But if you introduce an agent, like a detergent, one that can hold on to water molecules on one hand and hold on to hydrocarbon molecules with the other, then we can at least bring the two forms together, even if they do not chemically react.

Just as we sit at the intersection of tangible present and the intangible thoughts, we are also defined by other opposing extremes. This juxtaposition is the main cause of confusion in most of us, until we realize that it's not something to be confused about but rather something to be taken advantage of.

That's what we as humans do. We stand at the juxtaposition of physical nature and spiritual reality. Because of this duality we are exposed to, we are bewildered at the seeming bipolar nature of the two, convinced we need to choose one or the other to proceed. Untrue. We have access to both and that is why we can live an abundant life if we choose to.

Separating the Conscious from the Subconscious

Another area where we reside at the juxtaposition is the one between the conscious and the subconscious. Part of the process of the mind is known as our conscious mind, and the other part happens beneath the surface of the conscious mind. The design itself is pure genius and takes into consideration the speed of consequence and the nature of thought.

There is a speed limit to our physical world and as such, the conscious mind needs to abide by that speed limit. However, if all our thought processes were to abide by that speed limit, we would be in trouble a lot of the time. So there are some parts of mind that move at the speed of consequence to process what it has to, and then passes the results of that process back to the conscious mind for use in the physical world.

Because the subconscious mind can move things faster than the conscious mind, having the conscious mind monitor the subconscious mind will be chaotic to say the least because that would involve having the slower conscious mind inundated with the faster processes of the subconscious. Things that do not need to be concerned with the physical world like the processes to get to a solution can be relegated to the subconscious and the more present issues of the present world - your current time and space, can be monitored by the conscious mind. So its process is shielded from our consciousness. Can you imagine if we were privy to the speed of thought from the subconscious mind? We would be in total chaos at all times.

Our consciousness is the point where the conscious part of your mind intersects with the subconscious part. Again, we dive into this juxtaposition between two opposing extremes.

To be effective and to survive in this universe everything must be in balance. Imagine if you want to shine an extremely bright light on an object, you will not be able to distinguish its features because it would a complete white out. However, if you want to introduce shades into that object, the combination of light and shades create contrasts so that you can now distinguish the contours of the object. That's essentially how we recognize facial features.

The Human Psyche

The human psyche is the exact same way. Take for example the act of selfishness and selflessness. If a person is completely selfless they will not be able to survive in order to continue their work of charity. To be able to continue their altruistic work, a person has to exhibit some selfish traits. Take for example a situation in an aircraft flying at an altitude that experiences rapid decompression. Parents accompanying children are told to put on their masks first before putting on the mask of their children. This is a seemingly selfish act, but in order to be able to save the child the parent needs to be healthy and able. For that to happen, they need to put on their mask first, which is an act of selfishness. There is a level of selfishness in us that is then balanced with our selflessness. These two forces create a juxtaposition that is part of our character.

This applies to all the various forces in the psyche and each pair is in a constant tug of war. Equally matched, they keep the status quo until you willfully decide to move them in either direction.

So the question remains how does discipline play in with this talk about balance. Discipline is the arm that moves the psyche towards the desired equilibrium.

So we see that the psyche is all the combined forces of the mind. Each at a tug of war with its nemesis. You see this relationship in all the literature, except they are not spoken of in this way. Instead, they are often personified as good and bad. Your savior is discipline, aided by reflection.

Balance of Forces

A person's character is formed by the aggregate of all the factors mentioned in the preceding paragraph. Each characteristic is balanced by forces opposing each other. Imagine two colors, absolute black and absolute white. When the two come together in varying amounts, the black pushes against the white and the white pushes back. The result is thousands of shades of gray. Now imagine that shade of gray is your profile for that particular characteristic.

Each facet of human character, from thought, to responses, to empathy, to kindness, anger, everything - the entire gamut of the human condition is the result of a balance between two opposing forces. Where you place that balance, or to illustrate with the earlier analogy, what shade of gray you end up with is a function of your discipline. The resolve of your discipline determines where that balance manifests. It determines your character. To extend the illustration, let's say you have a light gray balance, and you determine that based on your proposed trajectory in life, you'd like to have a gray that is two

THE IMPORTANCE OF DOING IT

shades darker, then you decide to increase the black in the equation. It is your discipline that will do that for you.

Using discipline, a person can orchestrate a total character makeover. They can choose to become anyone they decide to, even become more successful, more loving, more healthy. You name it. Just by adjusting which forces to tip the balance in each facet of their character profile.

It doesn't matter what you're trying to accomplish. It's all a matter of discipline. I was determined to discover what life held for me beyond the inner-city streets.
~ *Wilma Rudolph*

4
RECOGNIZING DISCIPLINE

Most dictionaries will tell you in one way or another that discipline is the act of doing something that you don't feel like doing. That definition covers a lot of ground and within its imagery you get the notion that the effort to do what you need to is nonexistent when there is no discipline involved. There is some truth to looking at it that way, but it is incomplete. Because discipline covers thinking as well. You have to apply discipline to what you are thinking. Because thoughts do become actions when left to their own devices. It is discipline that moves fantasy into imagination. If you find that most of your thoughts are self-defeating or bias in nature, then you need to have the discipline to curb those thoughts and change them.

Discipline can be applied to both tangible actions and as well as intangible mental processes. Tangible outcomes refer to things that can be perceived by the five senses, while intangible processes refer to things like thoughts that go through a person's mind. Tangible and intangible form a dance that should be centered around balance but not necessarily constantly centered there. From a simplistic perspective, this definition would suffice. However, for the purposes of analyzing your career and plotting a new trajectory, the discipline that is required is one with a much higher intensity. Thus, it requires a more sensitive definition.

The Three Facets of Discipline

There are three facets to the discipline we seek.

The first is the discipline that aligns our actions to our rational thought. You can think of this as the discipline that gets you to move thought (noumenal) to action which manifests physical results (phenomenal).

The second is a discipline to hold our primal instincts in check. This is where a lot of us get into trouble. The idea of eating too much, for instance, is something that is within us. We need the discipline to move that equilibrium.

The third and final one is the discipline to think, cogitate and pay attention to what is real and what is necessary, versus what is not real, unimportant, or untrue.

These three facets of discipline, as simple as they sound, are some of the hardest things that a human being could possibly undertake to do. But with time and effort, it is very possible to achieve. However, if you are under the impression that this book will outline a series of steps that will magically imbue discipline upon you so that you wake up tomorrow morning with the superhero abilities that are attributed to discipline I'm afraid you're wrong. Discipline, just like anything else, takes practice. Work discipline into a habit and your life will be amazing. Any successful person you know or admire has learned this skill one way or another, and you can too.

Any behavioral change required to be installed in the human psyche requires two aspects to be accomplished, one is phenomenal the other is noumenal, as we have seen in other areas when dealing with the human condition. For the purpose of this book, within the context that we speak, phenomenal refers to things that are tangible and noumenal refers to things that are intangible.

Recall in the earlier part of the book, we discussed the energy economics that all of us have running in the background. For the most part, these energy economic methods are fairly spot on and serve us well. Imagine if you require 300 calories to walk from point A to point B. You are currently in Point A and your lunch is located at point B. You know that your lunch will only serve you 200 calories. If your body is fine-tuned, it's going to know right then and there, that that particular trip is not worth it.

That's the basics. Now add on top of that the typical inflation of the effort and diminishing return equation. The mind is left to calculate the possible effort and energy to execute the trip, and it is tasked with figuring out what the chances are that the energy source will be there when you arrive. If the mind feels that there is only a 50% chance, that equation is going to get skewed even more.

Now, this has been a rather long, yet simplistic illustration, but that is essentially how the mind works. We get lazy to do something because we inflate the effort required or diminish the return and compute that the effort is not worth it, so we sit on our laurels waiting for the next opportunity to come along.

Behavioral Change Using Discipline

To change this, what psychologists call behavioral change, is actually doing one of three things. You can either completely disregard the conclusion drawn by your subconscious, or your inaction, or laziness in this instance, and apply the effort to do it - this is blind discipline loyal only to acting on an objective; or you can change your thinking about the probability of the return; or you could think and reflect about the actual effort required and possibly automate, mechanize, or somehow reduce the necessary input - this requires mental energy expended.

So again, you simply need to change your thinking about the probability of the return. Often times if we can't see instant results, we tend to put off taking action, by simply being deliberate in how we think about it, we can change the outcome. Good things take time. Transformation takes time. Success takes time. In either case the various faculties of the mind need to be realigned so that the new equilibrium can be achieved. It is discipline, as we have seen, that moves this equilibrium.

One of the great lessons I've learned in athletics is that you've got to discipline your life. No matter how good you may be, you've got to be willing to cut out of your life those things that keep you from going to the top.
~ Bob Richards

5
PRACTICING DISCIPLINE

Just like the other aspects of the mind, there are also two parts to practicing discipline. You need to invest with tangible and intangible efforts in your quest to embrace and practice discipline. As with all things, the practice should come before the need or the opportunity to use it. You can't walk up to a piano for the first time at Carnegie Hall and belt out your favorite sonata without first having practiced it a thousand times or more.

In the same way, you have to first practice the art of discipline if you are going to invoke it in the other areas of your life. Practicing music, for instance, involves two parts - the tangible, and the intangible. The tangible is the learning of the notes, the learning of the keys and the timing and so on. However, there is also an inexplicable quality, the nuances of music that are not contained or transmitted in all the tangible material that is typically required, and it is what differentiates a virtuoso from a novice.

In matters of the psyche, there are also two areas, again tangible and intangible, that need to be approached if you want to be able to get the right brand of discipline to work for you.

There are three possible avenues in which one could accomplish this and it depends on your personal beliefs. For those who are religious this is the mechanics of Prayer; for those who are not religious this may be the mechanics of luck; for those who are neither, this is the practice of rituals. Of course these are broad categorizations and in reality, there are people that are an amalgamation of one, two, or three of the choices mentioned.

During the time of Alexander the Great, it has been recorded in history, that Alexander and the other generals were very fond of rituals and of asking the gods for favors before war. Whether you believe in these kinds of prayers and rituals is not the point at this stage. The point is these acts are intangible requests. In this case when Alexander prays to Zeus or when he prays to Athena, each prayer is a silent, intangible request.

After the prayer, the physical act of rituals where he pours libations or offers sacrifices are tangible actions. So you see the combination of the tangible and the intangible.

You will be doing the same to get started on the road to discipline. You will begin with the intangible act of embracing discipline and thinking about discipline in the various dimensions we have presented in this book. You will also look at the need for discipline and understand your need for it.

Once you have done that, the intangible part of the exercises is almost done. What you should do is keep it in the back of your mind and remain mindful of your intangible reflections on discipline. You can then move on to the tangible part of the exercise.

The first exercise for you to consider is fairly simple and is the exercise of fasting. If you have never fasted or abstained from certain kinds of foods, then this will be the ideal time for you to start. Fasting is one of the most efficient ways for you to locate your will to be disciplined, and you will learn to understand the temptations that test the power and resolve of your discipline.

The first exercise would be to fast in a way that works for you. You can fast processed foods, where you don't eat anything that comes in a box or bag, or you can fast from sweets or alcohol, or you can even fast from the time you wake up in the morning to dinner that same day if you'd like, where you do not eat all day. If you have health concerns please contact your doctor beforehand, but most of us can agree that fasting something unhealthy out of our lives certainly will not harm us. Whichever fast you decide to practice with, please keep in mind the importance of drinking a lot of water throughout the day. Fasting from something that you are used to enjoying takes discipline and once you master this first step, you will be well on your way to using discipline to your advantage. I once skipped dinner for 42 days straight. I ate breakfast and lunch, but I did not eat dinner for 42 days. It was challenging but I believed a higher power was helping me succeed. I attended business dinners, weddings, and even a weekend retreat, where I turned down eating and believe me it took discipline to do so. There were a few occasions where I came close to giving in, but I knew how disappointed I'd be in myself and that helped me continue on.

More On Fasting

Fasting is not just about religious piety. If you choose it to be that, you can. Throughout history, you see that fasting is invoked by those on a serious quest. You see Christ prior to the crucifixion, and you see Buddha prior to his enlightenment. Fasting is not the cause of the enlightenment, it is the tangible aspect of gaining discipline that is needed to achieve enlightenment.

When you muddle through all the myth and stories, there is a certain truth that rings through. When you fast, you build the strength necessary to deny your primal instincts and your deepest habits. That imbues tremendous strength in terms of being able to flex your discipline.

Aside from fasting, there are other ways that you could compete the tangible portion of this exercise. If you are a smoker, give up smoking for the day. The idea is to give up something that you ordinarily feel you must have.

However, fasting is the best way of doing it and together with your silent intention to lead a disciplined life, you will build the necessary power to do it, over time. This practice should be done at least once a week. Or if you decide to do something like I did, where you cut out one thing, it should be done once a month, or once every six months, etc. As long as you are proving to yourself that you can do it. As long as you are taking action and using discipline to enhance your willpower. The more you do it, the easier it will become and the more you will succeed in all areas of your life.

To practice discipline for the rest of the days in the week when you are not fasting, find an act that you can do on a daily basis. Something that you aren't used to doing or something that does not come easily. Walking, running and working out are all great ways to build discipline when you combine them with the intangible aspect as mentioned above.

Expanding the Practice

Once you get a grip and begin to understand yourself, you can move ahead and begin to practice discipline in meditation and mindfulness. Meditation and mindfulness are also not types of prayer, although they can be if you chose, but in and of themselves they are just a way for you to get in touch with your deeper self.

Meditation and mindfulness are also ways for you to expand your mental ability and to strengthen your mental faculties. This aids in the execution of discipline in other areas as well. Meditation and mindfulness are like resonating chambers where you apply a little bit of discipline and self-control and the more you practice, the more discipline you are able to bring to other areas in your life. Once you learn how to apply it, you will be able to use discipline in any area of your life where you want to get positive results.

Mindfulness has been misunderstood by many novice practitioners and it has been misunderstood by many others as well. But that is sort of a good thing. Because it is by mistakes that we learn the best lessons. As long we keep our objective in mind, learning by mistakes is valuable, for mistakes and their ensuing consequences are the best teachers.

However, as far as mindfulness is concerned we will introduce you to the essence of mindfulness and illustrate a couple of different ways that you can incorporate it into your daily lives.

Habits are generally not something you think of when you think of discipline. Discipline is more often than not associated with virtue, while habits are mostly associated with vice. However, if you are like me, and you have a lot of faith in the human condition, you will realize that every single attribute we have within us is there for the greater good.

Even making mistakes, is there for the greater good of learning; pain is there for a greater good - to prompt us to take care of an emergent problem. Every calamity you can think of has the greater good somewhere down the line.

With that faith, we look at habits in light of greater good instead of invoking the imagery of habits related to smoking, alcoholism, gambling and so on. We talked about that some in the previous chapter and we realized then that habits are just operations and processes that take place beneath the conscious layer of the mind. This layer can handle a significantly higher number of processes in a given moment and that frees up our conscious mind to do something else - like paying attention to the moment.

Once you have commitment, you need the discipline and hard work to get you there.
~ Haile Gebrselassie

6
SUCCESS AND DISCIPLINE

If you have no discipline, success will elude you and it will seem like you have no good fortune. Discipline is what gets you to do the things that are necessary in the pursuit of success. If you do what is necessary, then success is just a matter of time. The good thing is that all of us has utilized discipline in one way or another to get the results we wanted. You may have used it without being fully aware that that was what you were doing, but nonetheless, you were using it. Once you realize this and become deliberate with the benefits of discipline, your life can be absolutely incredible. Discipline is a tool, and you are capable of using it on a regular basis to fulfill your dreams.

In many situations, people make mistakes over and over again and fail in their attempts to be successful or build a life based on their ambitions. The made the mistakes, they learned from their mistakes but they still can't seem to make it work because they don't have the discipline to execute what they have learned. To many people, success is still a mystery.

Being a winner is not so much about hard work as it is about having the right mindset and pursuing a course of action that is consistent with the manifestation of the desired outcome. This requires discipline.

The psychology involved in putting one's self on the winning trajectory begins with the clarity of the desired outcome followed by the discipline to refrain from paying any attention to distractions that may arise along the way. Distractions are ever present, whether one chooses to be a winner, or one is indifferent, distractions are a part of life and they always will be. The sooner you learn to overcome the many distractions that life is constantly throwing at you the better off you will be.

There are eight elements where you must apply discipline to in order to jumpstart your success:

Mindset

Mindsets are everything and if you want to understand the psychology behind the winner, you are first going to have to get comfortable with various categories of mindsets and the means to mold them to your conscious desires. Molding mindsets are done with consistent work and unrelenting discipline.

The typical mindset required to be a winner is one that is constantly self-reflecting, and doing what is necessary at every stage. It is also not doing things that are unnecessary because time is a precious commodity when success is the goal. The key to mindsets is that they have to be neutral or positive - never negative.

Perception

You will also need to evaluate your current habits of perception, especially perception of yourself. Most unsuccessful people have a poor perception of everything around them. They can also keep themselves so busy with unnecessary things that they never reach their goals. In order to be successful you need to have faith that everything can go your way, and in the meantime, you need to see things for what they really are and then take action to make the necessary course corrections.

Now, this is a slightly complex concept because there are two versions of perception that you need to contend with. There are two because they are two sides of the same coin. The first side is the perception you have of yourself and how that contends with how you want to see yourself in the future. The second is how you feel others perceive you. That second one is a little complicated. It is not what others perceive of you - certainly not - because you can't possibly know what they see you as. Instead, it is what you think they see you as that has to balance the other side of the coin.

Reflection

The next foundation that you need, is the concept of reflection. If you didn't already know it, reflection is one of the key elements that every single highly successful person uses. They don't just do it weekly or sporadically. The true greats either do it daily or they are in a constant state of reflection. Reflection helps you to look at things the way they are and not the way you think they are. Reflection helps you to transcend notions and bias and if you do it correctly it helps you to see things that you ordinarily would miss.

So many times we think we know what others are thinking or why they are doing what they are doing. We make assumptions that just aren't true. We also think things about ourselves that just aren't true. It is finding the truth that will set you free. For spiritual people, the Bible or some other book may hold the truth for you. The truth is we are all powerful, capable, and lovable beings. We are all one even though at times we perceive to be separate.

Happiness

The next foundation is often missed but is a highly critical pillar, none the less, and that is the desire and willingness to be happy. Have you ever seen a sore winner? Or a sad winner? No. If you think that they are happy just because they won, you are wrong. The opposite is true. They won, and will continue to be winners because they are happy. This applies a bit to the Law of Attraction and I wrote a lot about that in my book "Get It Up: 101 Ways to Raise Your Vibration, Reduce Stress, Depression, & Anxiety, Increase Joy, Peace, & Happiness and Attract Abundance Automatically!"

Being happy is also a mindset and altering your mindset to include happiness, or completely creating a new mindset that prioritizes happiness, is not an arduous task. Mindsets can be changed easily if you practice discipline.

Strong Mind

A strong mind is a prerequisite to building and keeping the right set of mindsets. Not all of us are born with the propensity toward a strong mind. But that's not a prerequisite. It's a bonus. If you have a weak mind, and you will know it if you do, then your first task, before you do anything else would be to take steps to fortify your mind. A robust mind, able to withstand distractions, able to synthesize purpose, and willing to undergo pain, is what we all aspire to build for ourselves.

Being a winner can be about hard work if you like, or it can be about disciplined work. Winners are people who seem to handle gargantuan tasks with grace and ease. You don't see them sweating and groaning. These are the people who overcome the highest obstacle with the lowest struggle; magnify the simplest visions to gain the best outcomes, and do it all with grace and poise. And you can accomplish this with discipline. Successful people start somewhere and you can too!

Habits

Forty to fifty percent of all we do and accomplish happens because of this thing called habit. How we brush our teeth; the way we comb our hair; the drive to work; our initial response to unexpected stimuli, and much, much more are driven by processes beyond our conscious observation. For simplicity, we refer to the area beyond conscious observation as the subconscious.

Things like habits reside in the subconscious space of the mind while willful acts reside in the conscious space of mind. This willful discipline that's in the conscious state of mind has a counterpart that resides within the subconscious state of mind and that is disciplined habit - or an act where we used discipline to kick off what has now become a habit.

The great thing about habits is that they remove all perception of effort from the conscious mind and transfers the tasks to accomplish something to the subconscious mind. This frees up the conscious mind to do something else. Habits are key and discipline can become one of them. When you learn to create your own habits instead of letting nature and the circumstances around you form them for you, you will own your power and discover that you are indeed the captain of your own ship.

Character

Character is a combination of conscious elements and subconscious elements. We define character as the moral qualities of a person's thoughts, words, and deeds. Each person's character is unique, and they are unique because they are driven by different levels of stimuli when their character is tested. To illustrate, let's say the mark of character is a person not stealing money - regardless of how large or small the amount. The amount shouldn't make a difference.

An exercise you can do to reflect on character is to write out who you want to be. What characteristics to you wish to instill? Writing them out can help you become aware of who you want to become. Honest, sincere, faithful, giving, kind, responsible, trusted, reliable, etc. Once you know in detail who you want to become you can start acting deliberately. If you want to be an honest person, you must start by being honest.

Those are the eight characteristics that you can mold with discipline. Doing so will elevate your game to the next level each time.

It's easy to have faith in yourself and have discipline when you're a winner, when you're number one. What you got to have is faith and discipline when you're not a winner.
~ *Vince Lombardi*

7
A DISCIPLINED LIFE

And so we come to the pinnacle of our foray into the world of discipline - the Disciplined Life.

We form habits out of many things that come across our paths and into our lives. And we need those habits. For instance, walking is a form of habit. The ability to take one foot and put it in front of the other in rapid alternating sequence, while not falling down is a very effective habit. When you walk you bring 200 different individual muscles online. You don't really think about it, which means, it's like a habit because calling into service 200 different muscles happens beneath the surface. If you had to do that consciously, your conscious mind would be overwhelmed and you would go through life tripping over yourself.

But when you form habits in the cauldron of discipline, you then begin to align the best use of all that we have within the faculties of our being. Look at the layers of our existence. It's a simple three-step issue. There is the external environment; then there is the internal environment, and finally there is a boundary layer between the two. In the physical world, we can look at it as the ecosystem around us, the ecosystem within us, and the skin that comes into contact between the two.

These two environments have a profound impact on our actions, our thoughts, and the consequences that befall us at every step. What we desire in life, is also a function of our environment. Would you imagine that a native girl in the fringes of the Sahara Desert would aspire to a Gucci lifestyle? No. What we think is our internal motivation, is actually just something that we have come across. The native girl hasn't come across Gucci, therefore, she has no knowledge of it, much less any interest in it.

Whatever the motivation is, whether it's to live a fast lane life with an apartment on Park Avenue, with the latest German-engineered race bread car in the parking lot; or a contemplative life as a writer in the foothills of the Himalaya, nothing will materialize if no action is applied in the pursuit of the goal.

It takes significant effort to achieve things beyond our natural ability. A significant effort, both mental and physical, phenomenal and noumenal, tangible and intangible, that needs to be brought to mind and addressed. If not deliberately disciplined, it can tire out many well-meaning people who unfortunately try but fail time and time again and some even perish in the process. They literally work themselves to death trying. Do you know why they fail? They fail because they tried to achieve all those things that were needed to be a success in the conscious endeavors. That means they fought hard against habits that limited them, multi-tasked things that were difficult to do, sacrificed time with their families and neglected their health while the stresses ate away at their flesh and their soul.

But there is a better way, and that is the topic of this chapter - disciplined habit.

THE IMPORTANCE OF DOING IT

It is simple. We are all at this stage right now. You, where you sit and read, and I where I sit and write are both peas in the same pod. We've created habits along the way here, and although they may be different habits, they were habits that distracted us and robbed us of precious time. They are habits that have been formed without us really even being aware of them. When we realize that we are fighting back ferociously, because we are not getting the desired results, we also realize that we have been depleting our energies.

But here is what we need to do. Here is what the entire book has been leading up to. Ready?

Build a strong suite of discipline within you. And do it by practicing the various techniques of discipline. Instead of using discipline to annihilate your old habits, let them be, and use your discipline to bring in new habits that displace the old ones. This makes the battle inside you significantly less. Instead of battling old habits with the force of discipline, create new habits that displace the old ones.

What this does is it takes discipline and molds the habits so that when they do form, the habits are only going to propel you forward. Disciplined habits are stronger and serve you better. When you create multiple habits this way, and you, in time discover that every habit that starts your day is a new Disciplined Habit that you chose then you know that you are securely on a path to success.

God has equipped you to handle difficult things. In fact, He has already planted the seeds of discipline and self-control inside you. You just have to water those seeds with His Word to make them grow!
~Joyce Meyer

8
DISCIPLINE TESTIMONIES

In this section, you will find ten testimonies from people who have used discipline to reach a goal. You will find that you use discipline in many areas of your life. You might just not recognize it as such. There is power in knowing this, though. You have the power to utilize discipline whenever you want.

Try to think of a person you admire, or of a married couple who has a great relationship that you hope to have one day, or of a successful entrepreneur you think highly of, or of an athlete you've enjoyed watching. All of the people you admire for their accomplishments used discipline to get to where they are at. I'm sure they had days where they didn't want to get up and work hard, but they pushed through and took action. Day after day. And you have the power to do the same. Stop thinking of discipline as a bad thing. It's actually the very thing you need to grow and succeed in life. Change your perspective on it and your life will change. What an exciting concept! Read on for some simple things people, just like you, did to reach their highest potentials.

There is no magic wand that can resolve our problems. The solution rests with our work and discipline.
~ Jose Eduardo dos Santos

TESTIMONY 1

Hey Sage! Thanks for reaching out and asking me to consider a submission to your next book on the subject of discipline. I'd love to submit a story about how discipline has changed my life for the better. Incorporating discipline into my life has changed many things. There are so many things that have been positively impacted since you started discussing the subject of discipline with me that I'm not sure if I can narrow it down to just one thing, but I will try. The biggest way that discipline has helped me with is in regards to something that caused me the most pain I think I've ever endured. As you know I had an affair with a married salesman a few years ago. I didn't mean for it to happen. It wasn't intentional but I allowed myself to be weak and to give in to the temptation. We met online and he'd email me, he'd call me, we would meet for coffee, and he even came to my house at times when he found the time. I knew he was married and that his wife did not know about me, but for some reason I couldn't help but believe that he was my best friend. I looked forward to his emails and our long phone conversations. He worked out of town, therefore, he had the freedom that most might not have. After six months or so of conversing online and over the phone, we finally decided to have a face to face chat. I was so excited. I had grown to tell him everything. We had intelligent conversations that made me think in ways I hadn't before. I had grown to care about this man. A stranger who I now considered to be my very best friend. I had grown to love him even though, from day one, he made it very clear that he would never leave his wife. They had been married for a long time and he was committed to her. When we met for coffee that very first time, my heart was racing out of my chest. He was handsome and everything I thought he would be. A true gentleman. We connected like we had on the phone and it was a very comfortable and fun evening. A few months later he decided he'd stop by my house on the way through town, although, I don't think my house was really on the way. It made me happy to think he'd go out of his way for me. As he pulled up the driveway in his brand new Mercedes, I fixed my hair in the mirror that hung in the entry way and smoothed out my skirt. I was happy. My best friend was here but this would be the first time we were alone. As I opened the door his eyes widened and we embraced. Before I knew what had happened he had gently guided me into the house, shut the door behind me, and was devouring my mouth. I couldn't believe it was happening, but I didn't want it to stop. I knew how he felt about his wife, but I couldn't help but secretly fantasize about kissing him. Touching him. He told me that he missed me and that he wanted me NOW. I told him my bedroom was upstairs nodding to the stairs that were directly behind us. He pinned me up against the wall that was at the bottom of the stairs and kissed me passionately. I couldn't breathe. I felt weak as we both slowly slid to a sitting/laying position on the stairs. I was wanting him and aching for him to get closer. He slowly moved his hand up my skirt and I reached for his zipper. We slowly undressed each other as we made it up to my bedroom. We made love and it felt incredible. I hadn't been with a man in years and I had forgotten how wonderful it could be. As we laid there afterwards I couldn't help but ask him what his wife would think of this. His response was like a dagger in my heart. "She won't find out, so she won't have to think about it. I love her and would never

THE IMPORTANCE OF DOING IT

leave her or want to hurt her. I love my wife. Do I make myself clear?" He said while kissing my forehead. "Now let's do that one more time before I have to leave." He didn't wait for me to answer his question. Yes, he made it clear and he made it clear for years to follow. But I believed that he loved and respected me. I believed we had something special. At first I took what I could get, and was happy with that, but over time, the heartbreak I endured over and over just wouldn't go away. I knew it was wrong and that it went against my moral beliefs. I didn't want to hurt his wife, but I also found myself hating her at times. Times when I couldn't see him. My personal life turned into complete chaos. I was a mess spiritually, financially, emotionally, you name it. I was a wreck. And I felt as though it was all a result of the constant pain I was in. I didn't feel worthy, or like I even mattered, and I couldn't even tell anyone about my lover, my best friend. The only thing that got me through was learning about how to apply discipline. Oh I had tried to distance myself from him before, but I was never successful. We went six months without talking once but eventually I'd cave and email him opening up the relationship again. No matter how many times I tried, again and again, I'd be right back where I had been. Sad and depressed and in a deep dark hole I couldn't seem to drag myself out of. No matter what I did or how long I went without contacting him, I always gave in. I was in love with him. Once I learned that I needed to take desperate action and that I had the power to do so with discipline, my life got better. At first I decided that I wouldn't contact him for 21 days. I had heard that habits take 21 days to form. This meant that I wouldn't answer his calls or emails as well. And I had decided to delete his emails and texts without reading them. Let me tell you that took discipline. But I had made a deal with myself and I didn't want to break it. It was difficult, but every time I felt the urge, I would distract myself, with something I love, and tell myself that I'd rather be lonely and miss him than be heartbroken and feel unworthy. It was discipline that turned that 21 days into 42 days into 84 days into 365 days. Having been away from it has been healing and eye opening. After distancing myself completely from it, and working through it internally, I realized that the happiness I felt when I was around this man was not based on reality. It took discipline and will power but I did it once I learned what discipline really was and how to utilize it. Life is starting to look up now.

I love chicken fingers; I love French fries. I love desserts. I'm not just into dessert or just into savory food. I love it all. I'm a pig. I love food. So it takes a lot of discipline to eat healthy.
~Holly Madison

TESTIMONY 2

I used discipline to lose over 100 pounds! For over 20 years I struggled with my weight and couldn't figure out how to lose it. Nothing I did seemed to work. I went on every diet that has ever been invented, without success. What I didn't realize was that I was sabotaging my own success. I kept thinking that dieting was hard. I felt as though I was going without something. I felt like I was missing out. I felt like I was being deprived. I had to think about it differently. It wasn't hard, it just required a little discipline. Just like I had used discipline to form the habit of brushing my teeth every night, because it's in my best interest, I had to learn to form the habit of healthy eating and exercising for the same reason. I started out walking just 20 minutes a day. Even if I had to just walk in circles around my kitchen table due to bad weather. I formed a habit of doing whatever it took to get that 20 minutes of exercise in. Then I started doing the same thing with eating. I would only eat junk food on the weekends. It was hard at first to watch others eat cake and ice-cream and such but after a while, it became a habit. I started realizing that food didn't have to have control over my mind, body, and life! I started to think about it as a machine that needed good, healthy food that would help it work and run better. We should be eating foods that can give us energy and help us boost our immune systems. Within one year I had lost 100 pounds and it was all because I learned to understand what discipline really is. Discipline is a good thing. It isn't meant to deprive you; it is meant to help you reach your goals.

"We must all suffer one of two things: the pain of discipline or the pain of regret or disappointment. Discipline is the bridge between goals and accomplishment."
~ Jim Rohn

TESTIMONY 3

My husband and I took a class through our church called "Financial Peace University" by Dave Ramsey. We had been married for 15 years and had always been in debt. We also had a $2000 cash reserve allowance on our checking account which acted like a credit card with a high-interest rate. Although, we knew about this interest rate we always maxed this out. We were always very close to our $2000 limit. It's just the way it was. We had been together for 16 years and we always used this credit as if it were money available. We could never get it paid off no matter how hard we tried. Whenever we'd pay a little on it, we'd end up having to use it for something else. After taking this class and learning a few tools and biblical principles, we decided to try it and we had to apply a lot of discipline. It required forming new habits as well. After the class, and for the first time ever, we paid off our cash reserve! For the first time in 15 years! We also paid off over $14,000 worth of debt within one year! Something we had never been able to do before. We couldn't even believe how much we had accomplished because we didn't think it was even possible. We tried not to use our debit card, but to pay cash for almost everything, except for gas and online bills that we paid regularly. We also started to simplify our lives by cleaning out some of the clutter that had accumulated. We made several trips to the Goodwill. I believe in getting rid of stuff we didn't really need, something shifted inside of us. Our goal was to live a minimalist lifestyle, and although we are still not even close to that, I believe decluttering has helped us become aware of the little purchases we had been making. We no longer wanted to buy stuff that didn't matter. Before we'd go to the flea market or to a retail outlet and come out with bags and bags of stuff that we didn't really need. Now when we go into these stores we usually just browse and leave empty handed. We still have a lot of debt to pay off but we are getting there slowly but surely and it took discipline to change our habits. Now was are on our way! Discipline is not going without. Discipline is figuring out who you want to be and what type of lifestyle you want to live and doing it. Not allowing others to influence or derail you from your goals.

THE IMPORTANCE OF DOING IT

Effective leadership is putting first things first. Effective management is discipline, carrying it out.
~ Stephen Covey

TESTIMONY 4

I used discipline to change my way of thinking! I felt as though my inner being/higher self was telling me that it would be in my best interest to stop my opinionated, judgmental, and negative thoughts. And let me tell you, it took discipline to stop. I didn't realize how much I did it – judged negatively until I became aware of every thought I was thinking. I had read how some people put an elastic on their wrist and every time they catch themselves thinking negatively, they'd pull the elastic way back and snap it. This idea did not appeal to me, although I bet it would work faster than the method I used. I've also heard of people carrying a cutout heart and every time they catch themselves gossiping or having an opinion about something they would touch the heart to remind themselves to stop. What I decided to do was to apologize, ask for forgiveness, and then to pray for the person or situation I was judging. At first, it was almost constant. I couldn't even believe it. I knew I sometimes thought thoughts that didn't serve me, but I really wasn't aware of just how bad it was until I took action. I would catch myself thinking something negative and I would say "Divine Creator, I am sorry for thinking this way. What a man thinks, he becomes. And I don't want to think this way.

Please forgive me. Please help me think better thoughts. And please bless this person. You love them immensely. This is their journey, and I ask that you bless them indeed." Like I said, at first it was almost constant. I couldn't go five minutes without having to correct myself. Eventually, it got to be less and less. And I even found, after about a month, that I would just start praying blessings for complete strangers – those who, beforehand, I would've judged for some reason or another. It was an amazing feeling and life started becoming more joyful.

THE IMPORTANCE OF DOING IT

It was character that got us out of bed, commitment that moved us into action, and discipline that enabled us to follow through.
~ Zig Ziglar

TESTIMONY 5

Dear Sage, thanks for the message. I would love to contribute to your next book. Your book "The 2-Hour Vacation" was amazing and helped me a lot with learning how to think about leisure time differently. Life has been better since reading it, so thank you! In regards to the subject of discipline, when you first discussed it with me, I totally didn't even want to discuss it. To be honest, I listened to you, but in the back of my mind was thinking "heck no – this idea is not going to be for me". Just the word discipline made me shudder. All I could think about was being a child and getting disciplined for everything – from swearing, to picking on my sister, to chewing gum in school! No thanks. But when you explained it like you did – that discipline is really a tool that we should use on a daily basis to meet our goals and make our dreams a reality. I loved how you reminded me that all of the successful people in this world are successful because they utilize the power of discipline. Since then I have been using discipline in many ways and life has been different and in a good way. I started out with little things so that I wouldn't overwhelm myself. One thing I struggled with before was opening my mail. I know this sounds silly. But I never opened my mail. I would just pile it up until it was out of control. I would get late notices, and miss seeing important documents because I just never opened my mail. I've had my power shut off, my cell-phone service canceled, etc. All because I never opened my mail. Once my sister came over and said that she would help me with it. I literally had mail that was 6 months old in the pile! So I decided that I would open my mail immediately after bringing it inside from the mailbox and distribute it appropriately. So every day I made myself take the 5 – 10 minutes required to go through it and I'd file it where it needed to go. Bills went in my "Bill" folder. Insurance cards went into the "Insurance" folder, etc. There were many days where I thought I'll just wait until tomorrow, but I had made an agreement with myself and I stuck to it. It's been almost a year now, and I haven't been late paying a bill since I incorporated this new habit into my life. Something so simple but it has relieved so much stress for me. Bill collectors stopped calling as well. The other big thing I incorporated into my life using discipline is mediation. I had always read about the importance of meditation but I never made the time to do it. I wanted to, but never had the willpower to follow through with my desire. I started making appointments with myself and I tried to respect these appointments as if they were real appointments with health practitioners. If I couldn't make time in the morning, I'd make time in the evening. I'd sit in a comfortable place and listen to an online guided meditation. I felt myself relax and over time I noticed that things didn't upset me or frustrate me as easily as they had before I started meditating on a regular basis! It was amazing and I also felt healthier and happier than I had before. I definitely noticed a difference. But this new habit took discipline! It would've been easy to skip one, but I thought of it as a real hour long appointment in which I had to attend. This helped me succeed and accomplish my goal of meditating on a regular basis. Thank you so much, Sage, for the energy work that you do, not to mention your helpful books. You are making a positive difference in the lives of many and I, for one, am grateful. Many blessings.

Without hard work and discipline, it is difficult to be a top professional.
~ Jahangir Khan

TESTIMONY 6

I used discipline to give more. I came across an article on the importance of tithing. Giving a percentage of your income for the purposes of helping those in need. I had never really understood this concept. I was actually repelled by the idea. It seemed to me as if churches and charities were just out to get as much money as they could. Wow, was I wrong in my thinking. Giving actually helps the person giving more that the person receiving! So I started giving more in my weekly tithes at church. It wasn't the 10 percent that the Bible recommends but it was a start. I also starting giving to the homeless. Before I researched the concept of giving, I would worry about the person spending the money I gave them on things like alcohol or cigarettes, or even worse, drugs. What I didn't realize is that it doesn't really matter how the person uses your generous gift. As long as it comes from your heart, the Universe will take care of the rest. The person will feel your generosity, and the Universe will reward you tenfold. Once I started giving more, the easier my financial situation became. It was strange, but it's the truth. After I started giving more financially, the easier paying my bills became. Beforehand, I'd run out of money each week, but afterward, I found that I'd always have money left over. It wasn't easy at first, but each week it became easier. I also started volunteering my time at local food pantries and at church. There is power in giving. I believe that we are wired to serve and give to others. It's healthy and good for us as well. I told my pastor the other day that for some odd reason ever since I've been giving more, amazing blessings have been coming into my experience in miraculous, unexpected ways. For example, I needed a sleeping bag to go on a camping trip, but I didn't really have the extra money to go out and buy one. Two days later, my step-mother brought me over the nicest L.L. Bean sleeping bag I've ever seen. They no longer needed it. Another small example was that I had run out of dish soap and wanted to wait to get paid before going to the store to get some. So I was washing my dishes with hand soap to get by. And one day my mom showed up with five things of dish soap. Her friend was moving and didn't want to take them with her. She also had four things of laundry detergent and it was the exact same kind I use with no scents or dyes. What a wonderful surprise. Not only am I finding it not difficult to pay my monthly bills – which is so unusual and it doesn't really make sense since I am giving more, but little things, like I mentioned above, are happening on a regular basis. Things that I want or need are just coming to me and very unexpectedly. My pastor looked surprised and asked me why I thought it was "for some odd reason" that these things were happening. He then reminded me of several Bible verses that tell us point blank that when we give we will get exceedingly more than we could even ask or imagine for. One of my favorite verses on the subject (and there are many) is: Deuteronomy 15:10 – "Give generously to him and do so without a grudging heart; then because of this the Lord your God will bless you in all your work and in everything you put your hand to."

Many people think they want things, but they don't really have the strength, the discipline. They are weak. I believe that you get what you want if you want it badly enough.
~ Sophia Loren

TESTIMONY 7

How has discipline affected my life in a positive way? I used discipline to not use my cell-phone or go on social media for 60 days! My original plan was to see if I could go one day without it, but it ended up lasting 60 days. The first day was the hardest! What a habit it had become, looking at my cell-phone almost every minute of the day it seemed! Wow, I did not realize how much I was really using it. Once I got through the first few days, I felt more and more confident that I could get through another. I felt stronger and stronger with each new day and I even felt like I was getting myself back. It was almost like I had forgotten who I was kind of. I was so attached to that thing. It was freeing. Not seeing the drama that is usually all over the social media sites. I found that I was enjoying my dinners with my family and enjoying the conversation as well. I wasn't getting distracted by social media. I was actually giving people my full attention which felt great, but the downside was that I was now noticing more when others weren't doing the same. I was fully present during conversations with others, but they were not. They were still checking their phones and that was frustrating at times. Also, I lost the need to feel as though I had to check it every second. I told my boyfriend that he wouldn't be able to contact me that way, so he knew not to even try. Before I always felt like I was going to miss something if I didn't have my phone. If I left the house without it, I would go into a panic mode almost. But once I started not using it, all of these unhealthy feelings disappeared. It was freeing! But it took discipline. Once I accomplished it though, I knew I could use discipline in other areas of my life as well. Discipline rocks!

*In terms of instilling the values of
mental toughness and work ethic,
discipline is the gift that keeps on giving.
~ William Baldwin*

TESTIMONY 8

It took a lot of discipline for me to quit smoking. I had tried the patches. I had tried being hypnotized. But neither of these methods were successful. So I decided to take a small rock and put it in my pocket. Every time I wanted a cigarette, I'd just feel for the rock and move it around in my hand until the craving passed. At first, I was playing with this darn rock all of the time, but eventually, I found myself reaching for it less and less. But I know it took discipline. I tried to remember why I was doing it. For my health and for my family. I tried to visualize my lungs turning from an unhealthy black color to a healthy pink color. It took time and discipline but without the discipline, I never could have succeeded!

*Success is measured by your discipline
and inner peace.
~ Mike Ditka*

TESTIMONY 9

This might sound crazy, but I used discipline to be more sexually active with my husband. We have five kids and life is very hectic at times. There are times when, by the end of the day, I am exhausted and just want to collapse. Honestly, the last thing on my mind is sex. After getting some wonderful advice, I decided I would try to have sex with my husband every day for three weeks straight. I mean, when we first got together this was never a problem. Of course, that was before kids, but I've heard about other happily married couples who are still very sexually active and I want to have the best marriage that I can, so what did I have to lose with this idea? I had to change the way I thought about it, though. I had to set the time aside for this to happen as well. To my wonderful delight, after the three weeks, my husband and I were a lot closer. We laughed more. We cuddled more. We showed more affection throughout the day. Using discipline to reach this three-week goal, didn't require much effort either. Not really. It only took about 20 minutes (or less!) each evening and the benefits far outweighed the cons of that "lost" 20 minutes. It wasn't really lost time, anyway, because the results were amazing. Better than I could've anticipated. I have to be careful though not to fall back into the bad habit of just wanting to go to sleep at the end of a long day. It'd be easy enough to do. I have to remember how awesome this little experiment was and how much closer it brought my husband and I together. Such a little thing, that brought about such huge rewards. I would recommend anyone to utilize the power of discipline if there is anything in your life that you want to make better. You can do it and you have the power to do so!

*It is one thing to praise discipline, and
another to submit to it.
~ Miguel de Cervantes*

TESTIMONY 10

When you asked me to do a submission on how discipline has helped make positive changes in my life, so many things came to mind. I mean, isn't everything that has ever been accomplished by man been done so because they have used discipline to get the job done. People may not realize it but they use discipline all the time. Discipline to get up each morning. Discipline to get to appointments on time. Discipline to be polite and respectful to our elders. Discipline to go to work each day. Discipline to show up for practice. Discipline to scrub the toilet. Discipline to be responsible in all areas of our lives. I have used discipline, more recently to journal more, to start a prayer list, to read more books per week, to act on my intuition and divine guidance, to go out of my comfort zone even though it petrifies me, to clean my kitchen every night before bed, to re-wear my clothes more than once so that I will only have one load of laundry to do per week, to make a to-do list each morning to help me stay organized and focused, and discipline to do a 10-minute arm workout every other day. These are just a few I can think of off the top of my head. I usually write down my goals and then take action and do what needs to be done in order to complete the goal. I have read that all successful people learn to do this. I love goal setting and striving to become a better person and it takes discipline to do so, but the good thing is we are all born with the power within to do so. You have to take action, though. Just talking about goals and dreams won't get you very far. The important part of goals is the doing it part. Like the saying goes, Just Do It. Regardless of how you feel. You will thank yourself later. The importance of doing it is where it is at. Go for it!

Few men are born brave. Many become so through training and force of discipline.
~ Publius Flavius Vegetius Renatus

CONCLUSION

We all take discipline to mean something more than it is because we tend to focus on the method of practicing it. We see kung-fu movies and war flicks that show how discipline is instilled in the successful warrior. We see how disciplinarians use fear and authority to instill discipline into the mind of young students. And, we see the dry characterless nature of those who display strict discipline. We see all this and we get an entirely mistaken perception of discipline. But that's not what discipline is, as you have come to see in this book. Discipline is a tool. It is taking action regardless of how you feel. You are never going to feel like doing things that seem, or appear, to be difficult in nature. The important thing is just doing it. Doing what needs to be done to reach the goal.

To reframe the entire perspective on discipline we looked at what it really is in terms of how the body works. This is important because, for 40% of those who need to invoke discipline, the main reason they don't do it is because they have formed habits that are not healthy and because they believe the effort outweighs the outcome. This is something we all have to watch for.

What it all comes down to is that the primitive mind finds excuses to not do things even to the point of creating excuses and false perceptions all in the effort to reduce the level of energy expended on an endeavor. This is not a bad thing, and there is nothing wrong with you for being this way, it is natural, but this primitive mind can hinder our endeavors to become successful and reach our goals. In becoming aware of it, we can take action to change how we think.

Imagine in the days of hunter-gatherers, an animal would need to determine if chasing down an antelope was worth it and that he better have good chances of catching it otherwise he would expend the energy on the chase and then not be able to replenish if the chase ended unsuccessfully. This is the source of laziness, rationalization, and fear of failure even - the body's internal mechanism that creates impediments so that you don't chase down every red herring.

We also saw that the mind is constantly pitted against opposing forces so that it can find the intersecting pathway. Imagine walking on a path and you have an equal force pulling you left as there is pulling you right. When the forces are equal, you proceed along a straight line. If the force on the left increased, you would veer left, the same on the right. However, another way to accomplish the same effect would be to keep the force on the left constant, but reduce the force on the right. The net effect would be similar. That we have seen, in this book, is the essence of how the mind works. Our current state is always the balance of two opposing states of mind or forces.

Whether we are happy or sad, compassionate or indifferent, we are just a balance of the opposing forces. If our resulting changes from those forces is not working out in the environment we are in, there are one of two ways we can sort that out. We can either move to an environment that is conducive to our current state of equilibrium, or we can shift that equilibrium to acclimate the current environment. Either of those decisions involves the invocation of discipline. You can look at discipline then, as a way to change the equilibrium of the opposing forces in the psyche.

We tend to see discipline as either of thought or of act. But in reality, both are the same especially when you involve discipline. Because the act originates from the mind, either consciously or subconsciously. If you use discipline, then it's only the mind that you need to be concerned with. Because what we tend to call the body or primal instincts, is also located in the mind. We just feel it in the body.

There is a phrase in latin, "Bis vincit qui se vincit in victoria" and it means that to conquer all things around you, in essence, to conquer the world, you have to first conquer yourself. This conquering of self is the ability to change the equilibrium of the psyche and is in essence what we have addressed in this book - it is the discipline in you that conquers the world.

Yet discipline is hard to instill because it seems to be so widely touted as a hardship. As such the mind becomes averse to the very suggestion of it. Discipline is not a hardship or an inconvenience. It is merely the presentation of a new status quo that the body is not used to but in time, it will get used to it. When it does, it is called Disciplined Habit.

The element that we did introduce is somewhat of a mind hack. In most cases, people find that habits are the antithesis or opposite to discipline. And in some cases they are right. But through research, we have found that you can incorporate discipline into habits and by doing so you end up supercharging your life.

Imagine, when most people are spending their day in autonomous mode, constantly moving from one habit to another. Most of those habits are innocuous, some bad, and some accidently beneficial. Typically, we wake up as a function of habit. We wash up, have breakfast and rush out the door, also in poor habit. We even drive our cars in a habitual way. All of these are mediocre habits and routines leading to mediocre outcomes and pedestrian lives.

In conclusion, we saw that reflecting on what works and what doesn't, then creating habits that are forged in discipline makes for the best outcome. So instead of pitting one force against the other, we put them on the same side and that leads to success faster and with less wasted effort.

Discipline is a powerful force that is neither troublesome nor negative. Children raised in the light of discipline are better for it when they mature, especially if you teach them discipline in the right context. It is an unfailing ally and an unrelenting protector. Of all the legacies you build, and all the inheritance you leave your children, let discipline stand in the forefront. And the best way to teach it is by example.

Remember discipline is a mindset of sorts. Learn to think of the results as being long term investments. Everyone who has ever succeeded in life used discipline to do so and so can you! Utilize disciple as often as you can to reach your goals and dreams. You'll be glad that you did!

Now go and make your dreams come true! Become the person you were meant to be!

If you have other ideas or want to share your success stories, please feel free to send me an email at: sagewilcoxbooks@gmail.com

I look forward to hearing from you! Thanks!

ABOUT SAGE WILCOX

Sage lives in the United States with her husband of 15 years, children, cat, and dog. She is a certified energy healer and is working on becoming a Life Coach. Sage enjoys giving advice to her clients, friends, and family on healing, love, and relationships. She also enjoys studying human behavior, reading, writing, being outdoors, and enhancing her relationships with others. She enjoys growing closer to the Divine Source and reading and learning the Bible and scripture. In her experience, the more she learns and practices the Word, the better her life becomes.

Sage is a hopeless romantic! She strives to help others fall madly in love with everything about their lives! That includes all things most people would consider boring. There's no room for boring in Sage's life. She likes to spice life up in every way!

Sage has also written:

- *Love Letters from Exes: Proof That Life Goes On After a Break Up and Love Is What You Make It*

- *Get It Up: 101 Ways to Raise Your Vibration, Reduce Stress, Depression, & Anxiety, Increase Joy, Peace, & Happiness and Attract Abundance Automatically!*

- *The 2-Hour Vacation: Let Go and Relax, Reduce Stress & Anxiety, Gain Inner Peace, and Happiness*

- *Until We Fall (A Romance Novel)*

Please visit her website at:

http://sagewilcox.wix.com/books

Disclaimer

The purpose of this book is for entertainment purposes only. This book is designed to provide information and motivation to our readers. The content of each article, letter, or insight is the sole expression and opinion of its author, and not necessarily that of the publisher. The letters contained in this book are from contributors and are the contributor's recollections of their experiences. This is a work based on opinions, recollections, and true events, however, names, characters, businesses, places, and incidents are either the products of the authors' imaginations or used in a fictitious manner. Any resemblance to actual persons, living or dead, businesses, companies, events, locales, or actual events is entirely coincidental. This book is not intended nor is it implied to be a substitute for professional medical advice, and any medical advice and any medical information contained in this book is not intended to be diagnostic or treatment in any way. The author and publisher are not engaged in rendering medical, psychological, legal, or any other professional services. If medical, psychological or other expert assistance is required, please talk to your physician and locate the services of a competent professional. The author and publisher shall have neither liability nor responsibility to any person or entity with respect to any loss or damage caused, or alleged to have been caused, directly or indirectly, by the information contained in this book. Neither the publisher nor the individual author(s) shall be liable for any physical, psychological, emotional, financial, or commercial damages, including, but not limited to, special, incidental, consequential or other damages. Our views and rights are the same: You are responsible for your own choices, actions, and results. If you do not wish to be bound by the above, you may return this book along with a copy of the receipt to the publisher for a full refund.

www.ingramcontent.com/pod-product-compliance
Lightning Source LLC
Chambersburg PA
CBHW071519040426
42444CB00008B/1724